THE LITTLE GUIDE TO
THE BEATLES

This edition published in 2022 by OH!
An Imprint of Welbeck Non-Fiction Limited,
part of Welbeck Publishing Group.
Based in London and Sydney.
www.welbeckpublishing.com

ISBN 978-1-78739-255-7

Compiled by: Malcolm Croft
Editorial: Ross Hamilton
Project manager: Russell Porter
Design: Luana Gobbo
Production: Jack Matts

A CIP catalogue record for this book is available from the British Library

Printed in China

12

Cover photographs: Getty Images

THE LITTLE GUIDE TO
THE BEATLES

QUIPS AND QUOTES FROM
THE FAB FOUR

CONTENTS

INTRODUCTION

An introduction to the Beatles has not been necessary since 9 February 1964, that most infamous of dates when John, Paul, George and Ringo performed on the *Ed Sullivan Show* in New York. It was on this day that Beatlemania truly arrived on a global, televised scale, catapulting four unlikely lads from Liverpool to the world's first – and only – billion-selling rock band. "The Beatles saved the world from boredom," George quipped later, slightly underplaying what all the fuss was about. In the 50-plus years that have passed since that day, the Beatles' status as icons – gods, even – has endured. But with two of the remaining Fab Four now approaching their eighties, it's time to brace ourselves for the day when all that is left of the famous mop-tops is their words, music and bon mots. Of which there are lots.

I'd like to say thank you on behalf of the group and ourselves, and I hope we passed the audition.

John Lennon, 1970

So, this little book of quotes is a tiny tome that takes us back to a time when the Beatles ruled the earth. It is the perfect quick hit of that famous Beatle wit and the essential fix for fanatics of Lennon, McCartney, Harrison and Starr, which, last time we looked, was everyone.

Over to you boys...

CHAPTER

ONE

HELLO
GOODBYE

"

There are only four people who knew what the Beatles were about anyway.

"

Paul McCartney, 1984

The fans gave their money and they gave their screams, but the Beatles gave their nervous systems.

George Harrison, 1995

"

The Beatles saved the world from boredom.

George Harrison

"

We kind of like the screaming teenagers. If they want to sit out there and shout, that's their business. We aren't going to be like little dictators and say, 'You gotta shut up.' The commotion doesn't bother us anymore. It's like working in a bell factory. After a while you get used to the bells.

Paul McCartney

"
No, we don't mind. We've got the records at home. **"**

John Lennon, when asked at a press conference if he was bothered the band couldn't hear themselves sing at concerts

Hamburg totally wrecked us. I remember getting home to England, and my dad thought I was half-dead. I looked like a skeleton, I hadn't noticed the change, I'd been having such a ball!

Paul McCartney

Bang! He kicks in, and it was an 'Oh, my god' moment. We're all looking at each other, going, 'Yeah. This is it.'

**Paul McCartney,
on Ringo's first rehearsal, 2016**

❝

We don't like their sound, and guitar music is on the way out. **❞**

**Decca Records,
rejecting the Beatles, 1962**

> **"**
>
> I knew the words to 25 rock songs, so I got in the group. 'Long Tall Sally' and 'Tutti-Frutti', that got me in. That was my audition. **"**
>
> **Paul McCartney**

For our last number, I'd like to ask your help. Would the people in the cheaper seats clap your hands. And the rest of you, if you'll just rattle your jewellery.

John Lennon,
Royal Variety Performance, 1963

"

I always hate singing 'Twist and Shout' when there's a coloured artist on the bill with us. It doesn't seem right, you know. I feel embarrassed. It makes me curl up. I always feel they could do the song much better than me. **"**

John Lennon, 1963

There's a power in John's voice there that certainly hasn't been equalled since. And I know exactly why: it's because he worked his bollocks off. We left 'Twist And Shout' until the very last thing because we knew there was one take.

Paul McCartney

" We like it… or we'd be the Rolling Stones. **"**

John Lennon,
when asked if he liked being the Beatles

I'm really glad that most of our songs were about love, peace and understanding.

Paul McCartney

You have to be a bastard to make it, and that's a fact. And the Beatles are the biggest bastards on earth.

John Lennon

I was looking for a name like the Crickets that meant two things, and from crickets I got to beetles. And I changed to B E A because… B E E T L E S didn't mean two things, so I changed… the E to an A. And it meant two things then. When you said it, people thought of crawly things; and when you read it, it was beat music.

John Lennon, 1964

Many people ask what are Beatles? Why Beatles? Ugh, Beatles, how did the name arrive? So we will tell you: It came in a vision – a man appeared in a flaming pie and said unto them, 'From this day on you are Beatles with an A.' 'Thank you, Mister Man,' they said, thanking him.

John Lennon, 1961

I didn't do anything to make it happen apart from saying, 'Yes.'

Ringo Starr,
on early Beatles' success

I say, in history, where Queen Elizabeth I had Walter Raleigh, Queen Elizabeth II had the Beatles.

Paul McCartney, 2018

John and Paul's standard of writing has bettered over the years, so it's very hard for me to come straight to the top, on par with them. They gave me an awful lot of encouragement. Their reaction has been very good. If it hadn't, I think I would have just crawled away.

George Harrison,
on song-writing for the Beatles, 1966

"

We both had our fingers in each
other's pies. **"**

John Lennon,
on song-writing with Paul, 1970

It was like a tug of war. Imagine two people pulling on a rope, smiling at each other and pulling all the time with all their might. The tension between the two of them made for the bond. **"**

George Martin,
about John and Paul

"

I tell you, for every hundred pounds we've earned, we've gotten a hundred pounds worth of problems to balance it. **"**

George Harrison

Whatever way you look at it, the Beatles… and every other group in the top twenty… rely entirely on the fans. It would be no good finding a good song and making a terrific recording of it if there were no fans around to decide whether they liked it or not. **"**

George Harrison

Anything in this business is a fad. We don't think we're going to last forever. We're just going to have a good time while it lasts.

John Lennon

People only look at me as a Beatle, but my friends look at me as a whole person.

Ringo Starr

"

So, this is America. They must be out of their minds. **"**

Ringo Starr,
arriving in the US for the first time, 1964

"

I can see the Beatles sticking together forever, really. We've been together a long time. **"**

George Harrison in 1969

"

Brian Epstein was great because he said, 'You know, I think it'd be a great idea if you don't drink and smoke and swear at the audience while you're on stage.'

"

Ringo Starr

Having played with other musicians, I don't even think the Beatles were that good.

George Harrison

CHAPTER

TWO

BEATLEMANIA

We were a band who made it very, very big. That's all. **"**

John Lennon, 1980

None of us wanted to be the bass player. In our minds, he was the fat guy who always played at the back.

Paul McCartney, 1997

**   "**

America: It's like Britain, only with buttons.

"

Ringo Starr, 1964

We're not Beatles to each other, you know. It's a joke to us. If we're going out the door of the hotel, we say, 'Right! Beatle John! Beatle George now! Come on, let's go.' We don't put on a false front or anything. **"**

John Lennon, 1966

The basic thing in my mind was that for all our success, the Beatles were always a great little band. Nothing more, nothing less. 🞄🞄

Paul McCartney

If you remember the 1960s, you weren't there. **"**

George Harrison

"

The Beatles were doing things nobody was doing. Their chords were outrageous, just outrageous, and their harmonies made it all valid… I knew they were pointing the direction of where music had to go.

Bob Dylan

"

You go through life and never stop and tell your favourite drummer that he's your favourite. Ringo felt insecure and he left, so we told him, 'Look man, you are the best drummer in the world for us.' I still think that.

"

Paul McCartney

It was the simplest of ideas, but it suddenly made us one person — a four-headed monster.

Paul McCartney,
on Brian Epstein's idea to wear
matching suits, 2007

"

Everything's completely changed. We don't have a private life any more. And we are public property now. **"**

**George Harrison,
on fame, 1963**

Hamburg was kind of messy, having to sleep all together in one room — there was no bathroom or anything.

George Harrison, 1967

Lots of people have asked us what we enjoyed best… concerts, television, or recording? We like doing stage shows because it's great to hear an audience enjoying themselves. But what we like to hear most is one of our songs taking shape in a recording studio, and then listening to the tapes afterwards to hear how it all worked out.

Paul McCartney, 1963

Christianity will go. It will vanish and shrink. I needn't argue about that. I'm right and I will be proved right. We're more popular than Jesus now. I don't know which will go first, rock and roll or Christianity. Jesus was alright, but his disciples were thick and ordinary. It's them twisting it that ruins it for me.

John Lennon, 1966

If I'd said television was bigger than Jesus, I might have gotten away with it.

John Lennon, 1966

" Because I can't fit them through my nose. **"**

Ringo Starr,
when asked why he wears
two rings on each finger

We were told, 'You're going to film in the Bahamas. Write a scene.'

Richard Lester,
Help! **director, 1966**

"

We all had meetings about tax structure, and they would say, 'Oh, you've got to put your money in the Bahamas. So, when we were asked about making a film, we would say, 'Can we go to the Bahamas?'

"

Paul McCartney, 1966

Arthur.

George Harrison,
when asked by the press what
he called his hairstyle

"

Somebody said to me, 'But the Beatles were anti-materialistic.' That's a huge myth. John and I literally used to sit down and say, 'Now, let's write a swimming pool.'

Paul McCartney, 1965

Turn left at Greenland.

John Lennon,
when asked at a press conference
how he found America

"
I'm a mocker.

"

Ringo Starr,
when asked if he was a mod or a rocker

"

I hate for the Beatles to be remembered as four jovial mop-tops. I'd like us to be remembered as four people who made music that stands up to be remembered. "

Paul McCartney, 1966

"
Animation is not just for children –
it's also for adults who take drugs.

Paul McCartney,
on *Yellow Submarine*, 1968

I love him. Especially his poems.

Ringo Starr,
when asked what he thought of Beethoven

Anytime you spell Beetle with an 'a' in it, we get the money.

Ringo Starr

America has everything, why should
they want us?

George Harrison

CHAPTER

THREE

YEAH,
YEAH,
YEAH

We played… 'She loves you, yeah, yeah, yeah,' and my father said, 'Oh, that's very good, son. But there's just one thing. Couldn't you sing, 'She loves you, yes, yes, yes'?

Paul McCartney

There's always something equal and opposite to everything. That is why you can't say LSD is good or bad, because it's both good and bad. I don't mind telling people I've had it. I'm not embarrassed about it. But we don't want to tell anyone else to have it. That's something that is up to the person himself.

George Harrison, 1967

I think the four of us together, all sort of equal, make us one big whole. We're different from each other, yet alike. When you have a single leader and a backing group, you either take him or leave him. With four, you can associate with one of us and still like the rest of us. If you didn't like Elvis, that was that. With four of us there's more to go on."

Ringo Starr

It's become so easy to form a group nowadays, and to make a record, that hundreds are doing it – and making a good living at it. Whereas, when we started, it took us a couple of years before record companies would even listen to us, never mind give us a contract. But now, you just walk in and if they think you're OK, you're on.

Paul McCartney

We did think we were going barmy.

**John Lennon,
on LSD, 1967**

People just stare at us everywhere, as if we were a circus. I can understand it when I am Ringo the Beatle… but when I am Ritchie the person, I should be freer. I suppose I can't expect that. They've heard so much and want to see you. Fame, that's what it is. They don't realize we've stopped touring. They still want to gape.

Ringo Starr, 1967

Was the film really all that bad compared to the rest of Christmas TV?

Paul McCartney,
on _Magical Mystery Tour_, 1968

The way that Lennon and McCartney worked together wasn't the Rodgers-and-Hart kind of collaboration. It was more a question of one of them trying to write a song, getting stuck, and asking the other: 'I need a middle eight. What have you got?'

George Martin, 1979

Paul provided a lightness, an optimism, while I would always go for the sadness, the discords, the bluesy notes. There was a period when I thought I didn't write melodies, that Paul wrote those and I just wrote straight, shouting rock 'n' roll. But when I think of some of my own songs, I was writing melody with the best of them.

John Lennon, 1980

We've had enough performing now. I can't imagine a reason which would make us do any sort of tour ever again.

John Lennon, 1967

"

When it started with me and George, Paul and Ringo, we said, 'Listen man! This is a field of professionalism that doesn't need any qualifications, except that you've got to get down to it, and want to do it, and you can make it without a college education.'

John Lennon, 1966

I decided to write a song based on the first thing I saw upon opening any book, as it would be relative to that moment. I picked up a book at random, opened it, and saw 'gently weeps'. I then laid the book down again and started the song.

George Harrison

Life is an energy field, a bunch of molecules. And these particular molecules formed to make these four guys, the Beatles… I have to think that was something metaphysical. Something alchemic. Something that must be thought of as magic.

Paul McCartney

I'm the only person who is allowed to say nasty things about Paul. I don't like it when other people do so.

John Lennon

John and I went to Paris on birthday money he received from a relative. He must have been fond of me to spend that money. He let me have all the banana milkshakes I wanted.

Paul McCartney

They're like an old married couple with their kids. **"**

Ringo Starr,
on John and Paul's post-Beatles relationship

I can't speak for George, but I pretty damn well know we got fed up of being sidemen for Paul.

John Lennon

I'm in awe of McCartney. He's about the only one that I am in awe of. He can do it all. And he's never let up… He's just so damn effortless!

Bob Dylan, 2007

With *Revolver*, when we first did it, we were just really knocked out with lots of the tracks. But then, by the time the record is issued, we're a bit fed up with it and looking towards recording the new one.

George Harrison, 1967

Everyone keeps preaching that the best way is to be 'open' when writing for teenagers. Then when we do, we get criticized. Surely, the word 'knickers' can't offend anyone. Shakespeare wrote words a lot more naughtier than 'knickers'!

Paul McCartney, 1967

"
We were just trying to write songs about prostitutes and lesbians, that's all.
"

Paul McCartney,
when asked about 'Day Tripper'
and 'Can't Buy Me Love'

Everyone keeps preaching that I'm not going to try. I'll leave it to the psychologists and let them get it wrong.

John Lennon,
on defining Beatlemania

"

The rumours are too stupid to bother denying.

"

George Harrison,
on Paul's "death", 1969

The best thing about this group is that we all work everything out between us. It doesn't matter who is playing what. If someone thinks of something, then we'll try it. If I'm playing the drums and someone says, 'Try this here, or do something there,' I'll try it. The same with John on guitar... it's the same with all of us.

Ringo Starr

The trips to India had really opened me up. I'd been let out of the confines of the group, and it was difficult for me to come back into the sessions. It was a job, like doing something I didn't really want to do, and I was losing interest in being 'fab' at that point.

George Harrison

I used to have a hang-up about telling John and Paul and Ringo I had a song for the albums, because I felt at that time as if I was trying to compete. I don't want the Beatles to be recording rubbish for my sake just because I wrote it – and, on the other hand, I don't want to record rubbish just because they wrote it. The group comes first.

George Harrison, 1969

"

All of these rumours that the Beatles are splitting up are pure rubbish… because we're all great friends, and we don't want to split up. There's never been any talk of it, except by other people. **"**

Paul McCartney, 1966

Do I look dead? I am fit as a fiddle. I am alive and well and concerned about the rumours of my death. But if I were dead, I would be the last to know.

Paul McCartney,
on rumours of his death, 1969

CHAPTER

FOUR

JOHN, PAUL, GEORGE
AND RINGO

" The night we went to record 'Fixing a Hole', a guy turned up at my house who announced himself as Jesus. So, I took him to the session. You know, 'Couldn't harm,' I thought. Introduced Jesus to the guys. Quite reasonable about it. But that was it. Last we ever saw of Jesus.

Paul McCartney

Now that we only play in the studios, and not anywhere else, we have less of a clue what we're going to do. Nobody knows what the tunes sound like until we've recorded them and listen to them afterwards.

George Harrison

"

We used to have lots of ambitions. Like Number One records… *Sunday Night at the Palladium… The Ed Sullivan Show…* to go to America. I can't really think of any more. We're living an awful lot of them.

Paul McCartney

Their success in America broke down a lot of doors that helped everyone else from England that followed, and I thank them very much for all those things.

Mick Jagger

"

Two feet, nine inches.

Ringo Starr,
when asked how tall he was

"

What kept the Beatles head and shoulders above everyone else is that they were prepared to change, do different things. No one record was a carbon copy of another.

George Martin

"
Paul was the first love of my life,
Yoko was the second. **"**

John Lennon

The Beatles made it, stopped touring, had all the money and fame they wanted, and found out they had nothing.

John Lennon, 1970

We all have our special fans. If all four of us had to stand in front of a million fans, and they lined up behind the one they liked best… I think Paul would get the most. John and George would get joint second. And Ringo would be last. That's what I think.

Ringo Starr

There was a deeper love there that neither of us could admit to.

Paul McCartney, on John

We were fed up with being Beatles... we'd now got turned on to pot and thought of ourselves as artists rather than just performers... then suddenly, on the plane, I got this idea: I thought, 'Let's not be ourselves. Let's develop alter egos ,so we're not having to project an image which we know.'

Paul McCartney

By 2012, the masses will be where we are today, and Paul should be Jesus by then!

John Lennon

"

I have such an admiration for John, like most people. But to be the guy who wrote with him, well that's enough. Right there, you could retire and go, 'Jesus, I had a fantastic life. Take me, Lord.'

"

Paul McCartney

George Martin has gone deaf in one ear... now he can only work in mono!

Ringo,
on early sessions with George Martin

We'd get in the car and I'd look over at John and say, 'Christ, look at you. You're a bloody phenomenon!' and just laugh because it was only him.

Ringo Starr

And we looked into each other's eyes, the eye contact thing we used to do, which is fairly mind-boggling. You dissolve into each other… you would want to look away, but you wouldn't, and you could see yourself in the other person.

**Paul McCartney,
on songwriting with John**

"

I always feel blessed that there were four of us. At different periods in those early days, we all went mad, but the other three were there to say, 'Excuse me, come on back.' The solo artist doesn't have that. Paul still doesn't look at me as a Beatle; he looks at me like, 'Here's this guy I've been working with for years.' **"**

Ringo Starr, 1998

There's this revisionist history that it was all John and Paul. But it was four corners of a square; it wouldn't have worked without one of the sides. Ringo was the right angle.

Paul McCartney, 2015

Well, there'll be many more, but I don't know whether you can look forward to them or not. 99

John Lennon,
when asked by the press if they can look
forward to more Beatles movies

We do enjoy reading the publicity about us but, from time to time, you don't actually realize it's about yourself. You see your pictures and read about George Harrison… but you don't actually think, 'Oh, that's me! There I am in the paper,' It's funny. It's just as though it's a different person.

George Harrison, 1963

"

Non.

Paul McCartney,

when asked by the press if he spoke French

"

How long are we going to last? Well, I can't really say, you know. I can be big-headed and say, 'Yeah, we're gonna last ten years,' but as soon as you've said that, you think, 'We're lucky if we last three months,' you know. "

John Lennon, 1963

The only reason to be a Beatle is to make music. Not be in a circus.

John Lennon, 1966

"

I had a little school-exercise book where I wrote those lyrics down. And in the top right-hand corner of the page, I put 'A Lennon–McCartney original.' It was humble beginnings. We developed from that.

Paul McCartney, 2016

"

We had the whole floor in the Plaza, and the four of us ended up in the bathroom just to get a break from the incredible pressure. ""

Ringo Starr, 1970

I can't deal with the press; I hate all
those Beatles questions.

Paul McCartney, 1984

When John got with Yoko, she wasn't in the control room or to the side. It was in the middle of the four of us.

Paul McCartney

" They were a much better group than the one I was with. **"**

Ringo Starr,
on joining the Beatles, 1963

❝

Count the money!

❞

John Lennon,
when asked what he will do
when Beatlemania subsides

The thing about the Beatles —
they were a damn hot little band.
No matter what you hear, even stuff
that we thought was really bad —
it doesn't sound so bad now.
Because it's the Beatles.

Paul McCartney

CHAPTER

FIVE

TWIST
AND SHOUT

"

I said to Paul, 'I'm leaving.'

John Lennon,
on quitting the Beatles, 1971

Why should the Beatles give more? Didn't they give everything on God's earth for ten years? Didn't they give themselves?

John Lennon, 1980

"

I went off Apple during the heavy break-up period – I sent John Eastman in and said, 'You tell me what everyone is saying, because I can't bear to be sitting at that table.' It was too painful, like seeing the death of your favourite pet.

Paul McCartney,
on the break-up of the Beatles, 1969

John's in love with Yoko and he's no longer in love with the other three of us.

Paul McCartney, 1970

I used to think that anyone doing anything weird was weird. I suddenly realized that anyone doing anything weird wasn't weird at all and it was the people saying they were weird that were weird.

Paul McCartney, 1964

The world used us as an excuse to go mad and then blamed it on us.

George Harrison

There was no enjoyment in it. The music wasn't being heard. It was a freak show. The Beatles were the show, and the music had nothing to do with it. "

John Lennon, on touring, 1966

You can't top John. And John couldn't top Paul.

Paul McCartney

As far as I'm concerned, there won't be a Beatles reunion as long as John Lennon remains dead.

George Harrison

You know, I'm not one of these people that just because I've done all that I now become Superman. You can't touch me. You know, you can touch me. I'm very, unfortunately, very reachable.

Paul McCartney

"

It sounds ridiculous but it's not. I'm convinced the Beatles are partly responsible for the fall of Communism.

"

Milos Forman

I'm the only guy who sat down with John and wrote all those songs. It's me. I've got to pinch myself, I can't believe it. I just feel blessed to have known him and to have experienced his presence so intimately.

Paul McCartney

We laughed a lot. That's one thing we forgot about for a few years – laughing. When we went through all the lawsuits, it looked as if everything was bleak, but when I think back to before that, I remember we used to laugh all the time.

George Harrison

We were really professional by the time we got to the States; we had learned the whole game. When we arrived here we knew how to handle the press; the British press were the toughest in the world and we could handle anything. We were all right. 🙶

John Lennon, 1971

That's what the whole Sixties Flower-Power thing was about: 'Go away, you bunch of boring people.

George Harrison

I've got used to the fact – just about – that whatever I do is going to be compared to the other Beatles. If I took up ballet dancing, my ballet dancing would be compared with Paul's bowling.

John Lennon, 1975

There is not one thing that's Beatle music. How can they talk about it like that? What is Beatle music? 'Walrus' or 'Penny Lane'? Which? It's too diverse: 'I Want to Hold Your Hand' or 'Revolution Number Nine'?

John Lennon, 1971

I've got used to the fact – just about – that whatever I do is going to be compared to the other Beatles. If I took up ballet dancing, my ballet dancing would be compared with Paul's bowling.

John Lennon, 1975

66

I took from four o'clock to five to get home in the evening to the outskirts of the Speke estate and it was on that bus journey that I met Paul McCartney, because he, being in the same school, had the same uniform and was going the same way as I was, so I started hanging out with him. 99

George Harrison, 1980

Nobody controls me. I'm uncontrollable. The only one who controls me is me, and that's just barely possible.

John Lennon, 1980

The nicest thing is to open the newspapers and not to find yourself in them.

George Harrison

When we were kids we always used to say, 'Okay, whoever dies first, get a message through.' When John died, I thought, 'Well, maybe we'll get a message,' because I know he knew the deal. I haven't had a message from John.

Paul McCartney, 1984

"

The Beatles brought a taste of freedom, a window on the world.

Vladimir Putin

I lived in the suburbs. Paul, George and Ringo lived in government-subsidized houses. So I was a bit of a fruit compared to them.

John Lennon, 1980

At Woolton village fete, I met him. I was a fat schoolboy and, as he leaned an arm on my shoulder, I realised that he was drunk. We were twelve then, but, in spite of his sideboards, we went on to become teenage pals.

Paul McCartney

I couldn't put my finger on one reason why we broke up. It was time, and we were spreading out. They were spreading out more than I was. I would've stayed with the band.

Ringo Starr

We reckoned we could make it because there were four of us. None of us would've made it alone, because Paul wasn't quite strong enough, I didn't have enough girl-appeal, George was too quiet, and Ringo was the drummer. But we thought that everyone would be able to dig at least one of us, and that's how it turned out.

John Lennon

Ringo is Ringo, that's all there is to it. And he's every bloody bit as warm, unassuming, funny and kind as he seems. He was quite simply the heart of the Beatles. ""

John Lennon

Playing without Ringo is like driving a car on three wheels.

George Harrison

I hope we're a nice old couple living off the coast of Ireland or something like that – looking at our scrapbook of madness. "

John Lennon,
1970, when asked what he and Yoko
will be doing when they're 64

SIX

AND
IN THE END

"

The Beatles is over, but John, Paul, George, and Ringo… God knows what relationship they'll have in the future. I don't know. I still love those guys! Because they'll always be those people who were that part of my life. **"**

John Lennon, 1980

In order to put out of its misery the limping dog of a news story which has been dragging itself across your pages for the past year, my answer to the question 'Will the Beatles get together again…?' is no.

Paul McCartney,
Letter to *NME*, 1969

"
We knew it was coming, but we tried to pretend we didn't know it was coming. **"**

Paul McCartney,
on the end of the Beatles, 1970

The further away you get from the heyday of the Beatles, the more amazing it becomes. It's grown in stature. At the time, we thought we'd be lucky to last for five years.

Paul McCartney

At the end of the Beatles, I really was done in for the first time in my life. Until then, I really was a kind of cocky sod. "

Paul McCartney

The biggest break in my career was getting into the Beatles in 1962. The second biggest break since then is getting out of them.

George Harrison

"

It'll be nice to be part of history…
some sort of history, anyway.
What I'd like to be is in school
history books and be read by kids.

Ringo Starr, 1968

Ringo's got the best back beat I've ever heard and he can play great 24 hours a day.

Paul McCartney

Part of me suspects that I'm a loser, and the other part of me thinks I'm God Almighty.

John Lennon

I didn't leave the Beatles. The Beatles have left the Beatles, but no one wants to be the one to say the party's over.

John Lennon, 1980

"

The Beatles were a group made up of four very complex men – my small hand could not have broken those men up. They broke up because they'd reached an end; but in doing so they all created wonderful new beginnings.

,,

Yoko Ono

I don't believe in John Lennon the Beatle as being any different from anyone else because I know he's not. I'm just a feller. But I'm sure the Queen must think she's different.

John Lennon, 1968

The Beatles were just four guys that loved each other. That's all they'll ever be.

Ringo Starr

I definitely did look up to John. We all looked up to John. He was older and he was very much the leader; he was the quickest wit and the smartest and all that kind of thing.

Paul McCartney

What I'd have liked would have been the money and the hit records without the fame.

John Lennon

"

We were honest with each other and we were honest about the music. The music was positive. It was positive in love. They did write – we all wrote – about other things, but the basic Beatles message was Love

"

Ringo Starr, 1995

One of my great memories of John is from when we were having some argument. I was disagreeing and we were calling each other names. We let it settle for a second and then he lowered his glasses and he said: 'It's only me.' And then he put his glasses back on again.

Paul McCartney

I had no ambition when I was a kid other than to play guitar and get in a rock 'n' roll band. I don't really like to be the guy in the white suit at the front. Like in the Beatles, I was the one who kept quiet at the back and let the other egos be at the front.

George Harrison

More than any ideology, more than any religion, more than Vietnam or any war or nuclear bomb, the single most important reason for the diffusion of the Cold War was… the Beatles.

Mikhail Gorbachev

The first time I heard 'Love Me Do' on the radio, I went shivery all over – I couldn't believe it!

George Harrison

On paper, we're very wealthy people… it's just when it gets down to pound notes… then we're only half-wealthy.

Ringo Starr, 1968

We were smoking marijuana for breakfast. We were well into marijuana and nobody could communicate with us, because we were just all glazed eyes, giggling all the time. In our own world. **"**

John Lennon

"

There is such a mystique about the Beatles that they'll be expecting God to perform… and we're not. Maybe Elvis did the best thing by waiting a long time… [laughs]. Then they're so pleased to see you that they don't care what you do.

John Lennon

"

"

Paul was one of the most innovative bass players ever. And half the stuff that is going on now is directly ripped off from his Beatles period. He is an egomaniac about everything else about himself, but his bass playing he was always a bit coy about.

"

John Lennon, 1980

"

It's a lot of nonsense. Paul McCartney couldn't die without the world knowing it. The same as he couldn't get married without the world knowing it. It's impossible – he can't go on holiday without the world knowing it. It's just insanity. But it's a great plug for *Abbey Road*.

**John Lennon,
on Paul's "death", 1969**

"

"

Well… she's me in drag.

"

John Lennon,
on why he's attracted to Yoko Ono, 1969

" While everybody else was going mad, we were actually the sanest people in the whole thing. **"**

George Harrison